*For Gabe,
who first taught me
that I have my own
breath to breathe*
—K.A.

*For my
greatest teachers
Kurt, Ella and Viola*
—A.B.

Author's Note

When my son Gabe was 3 years old, our friends Carolann and Dany were getting married. During a pre-nuptial meeting with their minister, they were asked to list the 10 most important people and/or things in their life.

What a wonderful idea, I thought. So one night before bed, I asked Gabe to list the 10 most important people/things in his life.

"Oh, that's easy," he exclaimed. "Number 1 is me, then God, then Skippy (his stuffed dog), Huggy (another stuffed friend), you and Daddy are tied at 5, then Ba and Grandpa . . . ," he enthused.

"What's your list, Mommy?," he asked. He quickly interrupted, exclaiming, "I know your list, Mommy! I'm number one, then God, then Daddy, then Ba and Grandpa, Carolann, Amy, Godbomber (my best childhood friend, his godmother) . . ." and so on.

I appeared nowhere on my list.

Even at age 3, my son saw that I lived and breathed for everyone but me. No wonder I was so depleted, crabby and desperately trying to be seen and valued by others.

Now at 52, I am conscious daily to breathe my own breath, a giant (and, yes, I mean this literally, too) concept introduced to me by my beloved friends and teachers Jacque and Donald Nelson (www.themarygroup.com). Today, I move with joy, freedom, confidence and deep knowing of my wellbeing—all from a magical internal sense of me!

I invite you and your children to learn, feel and know the incredible, catalyzing breath of you. Don't forget to read Notes to Parents and Educators at the end of the book for more ideas on connecting to this magnificent breath of you and your thriving.

—Enjoy!

I breathe my own breath!

by **Kathleen Aharoni**

illustrated by **Ann Boyd**

Once upon a time,

we ALL breathed our own breath.

And we were ALL very well.

Then, we stopped. Humans stopped that is.
We held our breath, gave it away, and sometimes even lost it.

Nature continued to breathe its own breath.
And Nature remained very, very well.

We humans, though, became confused. We forgot ourselves.

We tried to breathe everyone's breath but our own.

We tried to breathe . . .

. . . Mom and Dad's breath,

which are as
different as
night and day.

. . . and Grandpa Gazunt's breath

that rattles and shakes like the exhaust on his car.

. . . and Dudley
the dog's breath,

which doesn't even smell very good.

. . . and Loquacia the librarian's breath,

which is very,

very,

very

quiet.

. . . and Feroshious the lion's breath,

which is very, **very, very** LOUD!!!

. . . and the breath of
Rahmanus the Redwood,
the most magnificent tree
in the forest.

. . . and the dancing breath of River Flo,

as she dances, bubbles, swirls and twirls.

. . . and best friends Jessie's and Gabe's breaths,

which already contain so many other breaths that. . . .

ARGHHHHHHHHH!

Call yourself back.

Breathe
in.

Breathe
out.

Remember your first breath.

Yes, you were very tiny when you breathed your first breath.
You had just arrived—sweet, slimy and starry-eyed.

Do you remember it?
Your very first breath,

the one that
happened at YOUR birth?

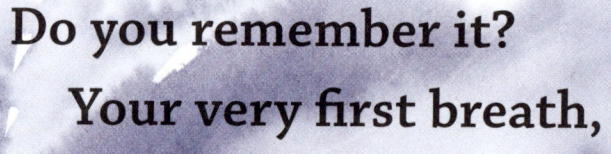

Yes, that's the one, your special, unique, one-of-a-kind,
nobody-does-it-like-me, totally-my-own, untangled breath.

Would you like to feel it again and always?

Close your eyes.

Look into your heart.

Breathe in. As you breathe out, say your name out loud.

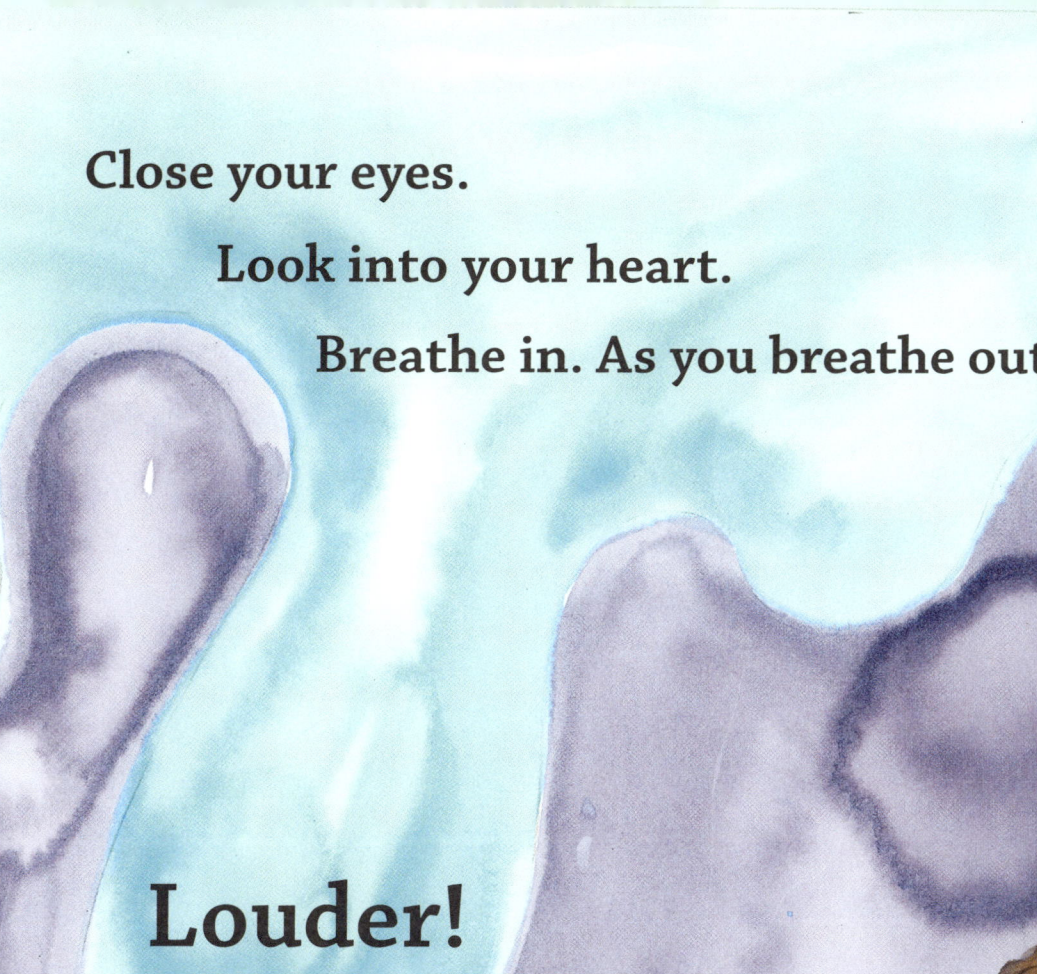

Louder!

(STOP! Don't take another breath.)

Wait

a little

longer . . .

Wait.
Wait
a little
longer . . . .

When you
can't wait anymore,

take a breath,
a deep, deep,
DEEP breath.

Let this breath
fill you from
the tips of
your toes
to the top
of your
being.

YES,
your
breath!

Feel it.

Is your breath warm or cool?

Does it explode, creep or whirl?

Does it have colors or shapes or taste like broccoli, bananas or squirrel?

Is it smooth like the blues?

Or vibe'n and twang'n
like an electric
guitar?

Breathe your own breath.
Mmmmmmmm. How does it feel?
Describe it.
Go ahead.

Take another
and another
and another.

I like it when I breathe my own breath.
I am a giant.   I am happy.

I am free. I AM ME.
And I am very, very well.

This is what my breath feels like:

Notes to Parents and Educators

Breath is powerful. And, breath is wonderfully playful, provocative and catalyzing. I invite you to peruse the activities below, use them or allow them to spark your own creations. I am confident that however you decide to explore breath, you will move yourself and your children/students to knowing and living their wellbeing, thriving and distinction. I am eager to know your experiences with the ideas below, as well as with the story *I breathe my own breath!* Please share, if you are willing, at ksaharoni@gmail.com.

- Breathe using the directions in the book. After you say your name out loud, continue to breathe following your breath with your internal eyes.
  - Feel the shapes, colors, movements, rhythms, length, etc., of your breath. How does your inhalation differ from your exhalation?
  - What aspects of you breathe—your eyebrows, nose hairs, heart, lungs, toes, fingers, elbows? What about your joy, gratitude, curiosity, imagination, wisdom and laughter?
  - Draw, dance, sing (like a song or a succession of descriptive sounds) or describe the feeling of your breath.
  - If doing this project in a group (classroom, family, birthday party), you might choose to make a mural that contains each member's distinctive breath. Teachers/parents might choose to participate, too. Note that even though they are older, their breath is of equal value. Breath is universal, and our individual breath is distinctive—not better or worse than another's, just different.
- Create a bedtime ritual that includes following the directions for breathing your own breath in the book. Follow with a few more deep breaths and then speak out loud one aspect of self that is distinctive and treasured, such as loving, playful, silly, creative, compassionate, adventurous, smart, athletic, trusting, happy, beautiful, confident, etc. There are no wrong answers. Remember to smile, tap your heart or blink your eyes whenever you recognize this distinction in your self or others during the day.

  This ritual can also be used in a group. For instance, to begin the school day, each student can take a breath and declare an aspect of self. This ritual reinforces self-connection and self-value. As classmates witness one another's declarations, not only will they be reminded of another aspect of their wholeness, their peers will witness their distinction. This ritual, whether done individually or as a group, is a beautiful invitation to the creation of thriving.

For more ideas/activities about how to connect to breath, go to www.kathleenaharoni.com.

ISBN: 978-1-59598-216-2

Publisher's Cataloging-In-Publication Data
(Prepared by The Donohue Group, Inc.)

Aharoni, Kathleen.
    I breathe my own breath! / by Kathleen Aharoni ; illustrated by Ann Boyd.

        p. : ill. ; cm.

    Summary: Discover your one-of-a-kind, nobody-does-it-like-me breath that celebrates who
you are and all that you can be. Includes an interactive guide for parents and educators.

    Interest age level: 003-007.

    ISBN: 978-1-59598-216-2

    1. Individuality—Juvenile literature.   2. Self-esteem—Juvenile literature.
3. Respiration—Psychological aspects—Juvenile literature.   4. Individuality.
5. Self-esteem. 6. Mind and body.   7. Picture books for children.

I. Boyd, Ann, 1965–   II. Title.

PZ7.A43 Ib 2013
[E]

Book design by Pamela Juárez
Cover design and production by Erin Sullivan
Publishing consultant Kira Henschel, HenschelHAUS Publishing, Inc., WI

Published by:
Water over Stone, Incorporated
835 West Buckingham Place, Rear
Chicago IL 60657

Visit us at www.kathleenaharoni.com or www.water-over-stone.com.